Gestational Diabetes Log Book

This log book belongs to:

_____

Emergency contact
Name:

Phone:

Address:

Date: _____

Weeks _____
Days _____

Water intake: ⬜⬜⬜⬜⬜⬜⬜⬜

Energy: ♡ ♡ ♡ ♡ ♡

Blood Sugar

		Before	After
Breakfast Time:			
Snack Time:			
Lunch Time:			
Snack Time:			
Dinner Time:			

Vitamins/ Supplements/ Meds:

Sleep (hrs) : _____

Exercise

Notes: _____
_____
_____

Date: _____

Weeks _____

Days _____

Water intake: 🥛🥛🥛🥛🥛🥛🥛

Energy: 💜💜💜💜💜

Blood Sugar

		Before	After
Breakfast Time:			
Snack Time:			
Lunch Time:			
Snack Time:			
Dinner Time:			

Sleep (hrs) : _____

Vitamins/ Supplements/ Meds:

Exercise

Notes: _____
_____
_____

Date: _____

Weeks _____

Days _____

Water intake: ⬜⬜⬜⬜⬜⬜⬜⬜

Energy: 🤍🤍🤍🤍🤍🤍

Blood Sugar

		Before	After
Breakfast Time:			
Snack Time:			
Lunch Time:			
Snack Time:			
Dinner Time:			

Vitamins/ Supplements/ Meds:

Sleep (hrs) : _____

Exercise

Notes: _____

_____

_____

Date: _____

Weeks _____

Days _____

Water intake: 🥤🥤🥤🥤🥤🥤🥤

Energy:

Blood Sugar

		Before	After
Breakfast Time:			
Snack Time:			
Lunch Time:			
Snack Time:			
Dinner Time:			

Vitamins/ Supplements/ Meds:

Sleep (hrs) : _____

Exercise

Notes: _____

_____

_____

Date: _____

Weeks _____
Days _____

Water intake: 🥤🥤🥤🥤🥤🥤🥤

Energy: 🩶🩶🩶🩶🩶

		Blood Sugar	
		Before	After
Breakfast Time:			
Snack Time:			
Lunch Time:			
Snack Time:			
Dinner Time:			

Vitamins/ Supplements/ Meds:

Sleep (hrs) : _____

Exercise

Notes: _____
_____
_____

Date: _____

Weeks _____

Days _____

Water intake: 🥛🥛🥛🥛🥛🥛🥛

Energy: 💗💗💗💗💗

Blood Sugar

		Before	After
Breakfast Time:			
Snack Time:			
Lunch Time:			
Snack Time:			
Dinner Time:			

Vitamins/ Supplements/ Meds:

Sleep (hrs) : _____

Exercise

Notes: _____

_____

_____

Date: _____

Weeks _____
Days _____

Water intake: 🥛🥛🥛🥛🥛🥛🥛🥛

Energy: 💜💜💜💜💜

		Blood Sugar	
		Before	After
Breakfast Time:			
Snack Time:			
Lunch Time:			
Snack Time:			
Dinner Time:			

Vitamins/ Supplements/ Meds:

Sleep (hrs) : _____

Exercise

Notes: _____
_____
_____

Date: _____

Weeks _____
Days _____

Water intake: ⬜ ⬜ ⬜ ⬜ ⬜ ⬜ ⬜ ⬜

Energy: ♥ ♥ ♥ ♥ ♥

		Blood Sugar	
		Before	After
Breakfast Time:			
Snack Time:			
Lunch Time:			
Snack Time:			
Dinner Time:			

Vitamins/ Supplements/ Meds:

Sleep (hrs) : _____

Exercise

Notes: _____

_____

_____

Date: _____

Weeks _____

Days _____

Water intake: ⬜ ⬜ ⬜ ⬜ ⬜ ⬜ ⬜ ⬜

Energy: ♥ ♥ ♥ ♥ ♥ ♥

		Blood Sugar	
		Before	After
Breakfast Time:			
Snack Time:			
Lunch Time:			
Snack Time:			
Dinner Time:			

Vitamins/ Supplements/ Meds:

Sleep (hrs) : _____

Exercise

Notes: _____
_____
_____

Date: _____

Weeks _____

Days _____

Water intake: ⬜⬜⬜⬜⬜⬜⬜⬜

Energy:

Blood Sugar

		Before	After
Breakfast Time:			
Snack Time:			
Lunch Time:			
Snack Time:			
Dinner Time:			

Vitamins/ Supplements/ Meds:

Sleep (hrs) : _____

Exercise

Notes: _____

Date: _____

Weeks _____

Days _____

Water intake: 🥤🥤🥤🥤🥤🥤🥤

Energy: 💗💗💗💗💗

Blood Sugar

		Before	After
Breakfast Time:			
Snack Time:			
Lunch Time:			
Snack Time:			
Dinner Time:			

Vitamins/ Supplements/ Meds:

Sleep (hrs) : _____

Exercise

Notes: _____

_____

_____

Date: _____

Weeks _____
Days _____

Water intake: ⛾ ⛾ ⛾ ⛾ ⛾ ⛾ ⛾

Energy: ♡ ♡ ♡ ♡ ♡ ♡

Blood Sugar

		Before	After
Breakfast Time:			
Snack Time:			
Lunch Time:			
Snack Time:			
Dinner Time:			

Vitamins/ Supplements/ Meds:

Sleep (hrs) : _____

Exercise

Notes: _____

_____

_____

Date: _____

Weeks _____
Days _____

Water intake: ⊔ ⊔ ⊔ ⊔ ⊔ ⊔ ⊔ ⊔

Energy: ♥ ♥ ♥ ♥ ♥

Blood Sugar

		Before	After
Breakfast Time:			
Snack Time:			
Lunch Time:			
Snack Time:			
Dinner Time:			

Vitamins/ Supplements/ Meds:

Sleep (hrs) : _____

Exercise

Notes: _____
_____
_____

Date: _____

Weeks _____

Days _____

Water intake: 🥛 🥛 🥛 🥛 🥛 🥛 🥛 🥛

Energy: ♥ ♥ ♥ ♥ ♥

		Blood Sugar	
		Before	After
Breakfast Time:			
Snack Time:			
Lunch Time:			
Snack Time:			
Dinner Time:			

Vitamins/ Supplements/ Meds:

Sleep (hrs) : _____

Exercise

Notes: _____

Date: _____

Weeks _____
Days _____

Water intake: 🥤🥤🥤🥤🥤🥤🥤🥤

Energy: 🤍❤️🤍❤️🤍❤️

		Blood Sugar	
		Before	After
Breakfast Time:			
Snack Time:			
Lunch Time:			
Snack Time:			
Dinner Time:			

Vitamins/ Supplements/ Meds:

Sleep (hrs) : _____

Exercise

Notes: _____
_____
_____

Date: _____

Weeks _____
Days _____

Water intake: ⊔ ⊔ ⊔ ⊔ ⊔ ⊔ ⊔

Energy: ♥ ♥ ♥ ♥ ♥

Blood Sugar

		Before	After
Breakfast Time:			
Snack Time:			
Lunch Time:			
Snack Time:			
Dinner Time:			

Vitamins/ Supplements/ Meds:

Sleep (hrs) : _____

Exercise

Notes: _____
_____

Date: _____

Weeks _____
Days _____

Water intake: 🥤🥤🥤🥤🥤🥤🥤

Energy: 🖤🖤🖤🖤🖤🖤

Blood Sugar

		Before	After
Breakfast Time:			
Snack Time:			
Lunch Time:			
Snack Time:			
Dinner Time:			

Vitamins/ Supplements/ Meds:

Sleep (hrs) : _____

Exercise

Notes: _____
_____
_____

Date: _____

Weeks _____
Days _____

Water intake: 🥛 🥛 🥛 🥛 🥛 🥛 🥛

Energy: 🧡 🧡 🧡 🧡 🧡

		Blood Sugar	
		Before	After
Breakfast Time:			
Snack Time:			
Lunch Time:			
Snack Time:			
Dinner Time:			

Vitamins/ Supplements/ Meds:

Sleep (hrs) : _____

Exercise

Notes: _____

_____

_____

Date: _____

Weeks _____
Days _____

Water intake: ⑁ ⑁ ⑁ ⑁ ⑁ ⑁ ⑁

Energy: ♥ ♥ ♥ ♥ ♥

Blood Sugar

		Before	After
Breakfast Time:			
Snack Time:			
Lunch Time:			
Snack Time:			
Dinner Time:			

Vitamins/ Supplements/ Meds:

Sleep (hrs) : _____

Exercise

Notes: _____
_____
_____

Date: _____

Weeks _____
Days _____

Water intake: 🥛 🥛 🥛 🥛 🥛 🥛 🥛 🥛

Energy: 🤍 🤍 🤍 🤍 🤍

		Blood Sugar	
		Before	After
Breakfast Time:			
Snack Time:			
Lunch Time:			
Snack Time:			
Dinner Time:			

Vitamins/ Supplements/ Meds:

Sleep (hrs) : _____

Exercise

Notes: _____

_____

_____

Date: _____

Weeks _____

Days _____

Water intake: ☐ ☐ ☐ ☐ ☐ ☐ ☐ ☐

Energy: ♥ ♥ ♥ ♥ ♥ ♥

		Blood Sugar	
		Before	After
Breakfast Time:			
Snack Time:			
Lunch Time:			
Snack Time:			
Dinner Time:			

Vitamins/ Supplements/ Meds:

Sleep (hrs) : _____

Exercise

Notes: _____
_____
_____

Date: _____

Weeks _____
Days _____

Water intake: ⬚ ⬚ ⬚ ⬚ ⬚ ⬚ ⬚ ⬚

Energy: ♡ ♡ ♡ ♡ ♡ ♡

Blood Sugar

		Before	After
Breakfast Time:			
Snack Time:			
Lunch Time:			
Snack Time:			
Dinner Time:			

Vitamins/ Supplements/ Meds:

Sleep (hrs) : _____

Exercise

Notes: _____
_____
_____

Date: _____

Weeks _____

Days _____

Water intake: 🥛🥛🥛🥛🥛🥛🥛

Energy: 💜💜💜💜💜

Blood Sugar

		Before	After
Breakfast Time:			
Snack Time:			
Lunch Time:			
Snack Time:			
Dinner Time:			

Vitamins/ Supplements/ Meds:

Sleep (hrs) : _____

Exercise

Notes: _____
_____
_____

Date: _____

Weeks _____
Days _____

Water intake: 🥛 🥛 🥛 🥛 🥛 🥛 🥛

Energy: ♡ ♡ ♡ ♡ ♡

		Blood Sugar	
		Before	After
Breakfast Time:			
Snack Time:			
Lunch Time:			
Snack Time:			
Dinner Time:			

Vitamins/ Supplements/ Meds:

Sleep (hrs) : _____

Exercise

Notes: _____

_____

_____

Date: _____

Weeks _____
Days _____

Water intake: ⬛⬛⬛⬛⬛⬛⬛⬛

Energy: ♥♥♥♥♥♥

Blood Sugar

		Before	After
Breakfast Time:			
Snack Time:			
Lunch Time:			
Snack Time:			
Dinner Time:			

Vitamins/ Supplements/ Meds:

Sleep (hrs) : _____

Exercise

Notes: _____
_____
_____

Date: _____

Weeks _____

Days _____

Water intake: ⬚ ⬚ ⬚ ⬚ ⬚ ⬚ ⬚ ⬚

Energy: ♥ ♥ ♥ ♥ ♥

		Blood Sugar	
		Before	After
Breakfast Time:			
Snack Time:			
Lunch Time:			
Snack Time:			
Dinner Time:			

Vitamins/ Supplements/ Meds:

Sleep (hrs) : _____

Exercise

Notes: _____

_____

_____

Date: _____

Weeks _____

Days _____

Water intake: ▯ ▯ ▯ ▯ ▯ ▯ ▯

Energy: ♥ ♥ ♥ ♥ ♥

Blood Sugar

		Before	After
Breakfast Time:			
Snack Time:			
Lunch Time:			
Snack Time:			
Dinner Time:			

Vitamins/ Supplements/ Meds:

Sleep (hrs) : _____

Exercise

Notes: _____
_____
_____

Date: _____

Weeks _____

Water intake: ⎕ ⎕ ⎕ ⎕ ⎕ ⎕ ⎕

Days _____

Energy: ♥♥ ♥♥ ♥♥ ♥♥ ♥♥

		Blood Sugar	
		Before	After
Breakfast Time:			
Snack Time:			
Lunch Time:			
Snack Time:			
Dinner Time:			

Vitamins/ Supplements/ Meds:

Sleep (hrs) : _____

Exercise

Notes: _____

_____

_____

Date: _____

Weeks _____
Days _____

Water intake: ⊓ ⊓ ⊓ ⊓ ⊓ ⊓ ⊓

Energy: 💜 💜 💜 💜 💜 💜

Blood Sugar

		Before	After
Breakfast Time:			
Snack Time:			
Lunch Time:			
Snack Time:			
Dinner Time:			

Vitamins/ Supplements/ Meds:

Sleep (hrs) : _____

Exercise

Notes: _____
_____
_____

Date: _____

Weeks _____

Days _____

Water intake: 🥤🥤🥤🥤🥤🥤🥤

Energy: 💜💜💜💜💜💜

Blood Sugar

		Before	After
Breakfast Time:			
Snack Time:			
Lunch Time:			
Snack Time:			
Dinner Time:			

Vitamins/ Supplements/ Meds:

Sleep (hrs) : _____

Exercise

Notes: _____

_____

_____

Date: _____

Weeks _____
Days _____

Water intake: 🥤🥤🥤🥤🥤🥤🥤

Energy: 🩶🩶🩶🩶🩶

Blood Sugar

		Before	After
Breakfast Time:			
Snack Time:			
Lunch Time:			
Snack Time:			
Dinner Time:			

Vitamins/ Supplements/ Meds:

Sleep (hrs) : _____

Exercise

Notes: _____
_____
_____

Date: _____

Weeks _____

Days _____

Water intake: ⬜⬜⬜⬜⬜⬜⬜⬜

Energy: ♡♡♡♡♡

Blood Sugar

		Before	After
Breakfast Time:			
Snack Time:			
Lunch Time:			
Snack Time:			
Dinner Time:			

Vitamins/ Supplements/ Meds:

Sleep (hrs) : _____

Exercise

Notes: _____

Date: _____

Weeks _____

Days _____

Water intake: 🥤🥤🥤🥤🥤🥤🥤🥤

Energy: 💜💜💜💜💜💜

		Blood Sugar	
		Before	After
Breakfast Time:			
Snack Time:			
Lunch Time:			
Snack Time:			
Dinner Time:			

Vitamins/ Supplements/ Meds:

Sleep (hrs) : _____

Exercise

Notes: _____
_____
_____

Date: _____

Weeks _____

Days _____

Water intake: ⊔ ⊔ ⊔ ⊔ ⊔ ⊔ ⊔

Energy: ♡ ♡ ♡ ♡ ♡

Blood Sugar

		Before	After
Breakfast Time:			
Snack Time:			
Lunch Time:			
Snack Time:			
Dinner Time:			

Vitamins/ Supplements/ Meds:

Sleep (hrs) : _____

Exercise

Notes: _____

Date: _____

Weeks _____

Days _____

Water intake: ⬜ ⬜ ⬜ ⬜ ⬜ ⬜ ⬜ ⬜

Energy: 🩶 🩶 🩶 🩶 🩶 🩶

Blood Sugar

		Before	After
Breakfast Time:			
Snack Time:			
Lunch Time:			
Snack Time:			
Dinner Time:			

Vitamins/ Supplements/ Meds:

Sleep (hrs) : _____

Exercise

Notes: _____
_____
_____

Date: _____

Weeks _____

Days _____

Water intake: ⛾ ⛾ ⛾ ⛾ ⛾ ⛾ ⛾

Energy: ♥ ♥ ♥ ♥ ♥ ♥

Blood Sugar

		Before	After
Breakfast Time:			
Snack Time:			
Lunch Time:			
Snack Time:			
Dinner Time:			

Vitamins/ Supplements/ Meds:

Sleep (hrs) : _____

Exercise

Notes:

_____

Date: _____

Weeks _____
Days _____

Water intake: 🥛🥛🥛🥛🥛🥛🥛🥛🥛

Energy: 🤍🤍🤍🤍🤍

Blood Sugar

		Before	After
Breakfast Time:			
Snack Time:			
Lunch Time:			
Snack Time:			
Dinner Time:			

Vitamins/ Supplements/ Meds:

Sleep (hrs) : _____

Exercise

Notes: _____
_____
_____

Date: _____

Weeks _____

Days _____

Water intake: ⬜⬜⬜⬜⬜⬜⬜⬜

Energy: ♡♡ ♡♡ ♡♡ ♡♡ ♡♡

		Blood Sugar	
		Before	After
Breakfast Time:			
Snack Time:			
Lunch Time:			
Snack Time:			
Dinner Time:			

Vitamins/ Supplements/ Meds:

Sleep (hrs) : _____

Exercise

Notes: _____

_____

_____

Date: _____

Weeks _____
Days _____

Water intake: ⬜⬜⬜⬜⬜⬜⬜

Energy: 🩶🩶🩶🩶🩶

Blood Sugar

		Before	After
Breakfast Time:			
Snack Time:			
Lunch Time:			
Snack Time:			
Dinner Time:			

Vitamins/ Supplements/ Meds:

Sleep (hrs) : _____

Exercise

Notes: _____
_____
_____

Date: _____

Weeks _____

Days _____

Water intake: ⊔ ⊔ ⊔ ⊔ ⊔ ⊔ ⊔

Energy: ♡ ♡ ♡ ♡ ♡

Blood Sugar

		Before	After
Breakfast Time:			
Snack Time:			
Lunch Time:			
Snack Time:			
Dinner Time:			

Vitamins/ Supplements/ Meds:

Sleep (hrs) : _____

Exercise

Notes: _____
_____
_____

Date: _____

Weeks _____

Days _____

Water intake: ⬜⬜⬜⬜⬜⬜⬜

Energy: 🤍🤍🤍🤍🤍

Blood Sugar

		Before	After
Breakfast Time:			
Snack Time:			
Lunch Time:			
Snack Time:			
Dinner Time:			

Vitamins/ Supplements/ Meds:

Sleep (hrs) : _____

Exercise

Notes: _____
_____
_____

Date: _____

Weeks _____

Days _____

Water intake: 🥤🥤🥤🥤🥤🥤🥤

Energy: 💗💗💗💗💗💗

		Blood Sugar	
		Before	After
Breakfast Time:			
Snack Time:			
Lunch Time:			
Snack Time:			
Dinner Time:			

Vitamins/ Supplements/ Meds:

Sleep (hrs) : _____

Exercise

Notes: _____

_____

_____

Date: _____

Weeks _____

Days _____

Water intake: ▯ ▯ ▯ ▯ ▯ ▯ ▯

Energy: ♥ ♥ ♥ ♥ ♥

Blood Sugar

		Before	After
Breakfast Time:			
Snack Time:			
Lunch Time:			
Snack Time:			
Dinner Time:			

Vitamins/ Supplements/ Meds:

Sleep (hrs) : _____

Exercise

Notes: _____
_____
_____

Date: _____

Weeks _____

Days _____

Water intake: ⊔ ⊔ ⊔ ⊔ ⊔ ⊔ ⊔ ⊔

Energy: ♡ ♡ ♡ ♡ ♡

		Blood Sugar	
		Before	After
Breakfast Time:			
Snack Time:			
Lunch Time:			
Snack Time:			
Dinner Time:			

Vitamins/ Supplements/ Meds:

Sleep (hrs) : _____

Exercise

Notes: _____

_____

_____

Date: _____

Weeks _____
Days _____

Water intake: ⛾ ⛾ ⛾ ⛾ ⛾ ⛾ ⛾ ⛾

Energy: ♥ ♥ ♥ ♥ ♥

Blood Sugar

		Before	After
Breakfast Time:			
Snack Time:			
Lunch Time:			
Snack Time:			
Dinner Time:			

Vitamins/ Supplements/ Meds:

Sleep (hrs) : _____

Exercise

Notes: _____
_____
_____

Date: _____

Weeks _____

Days _____

Water intake: 🥛🥛🥛🥛🥛🥛🥛

Energy: ♥♥♥♥♥♥

Blood Sugar

		Before	After
Breakfast Time:			
Snack Time:			
Lunch Time:			
Snack Time:			
Dinner Time:			

Vitamins/ Supplements/ Meds:

Sleep (hrs) : _____

Exercise

Notes: _____
_____
_____

Date: _____

Weeks _____

Days _____

Water intake: ⊔ ⊔ ⊔ ⊔ ⊔ ⊔ ⊔

Energy: ♡ ♡ ♡ ♡ ♡

Blood Sugar

		Before	After
Breakfast Time:			
Snack Time:			
Lunch Time:			
Snack Time:			
Dinner Time:			

Vitamins/ Supplements/ Meds:

Sleep (hrs) : _____

Exercise

Notes: _____

Date: _____

Weeks _____
Days _____

Water intake: 🥛🥛🥛🥛🥛🥛🥛

Energy:

		Before	After
Breakfast Time:			
Snack Time:			
Lunch Time:			
Snack Time:			
Dinner Time:			

Vitamins/ Supplements/ Meds:

Sleep (hrs) : _____

Exercise

Notes: _____
_____
_____

Date: _____

Weeks _____
Days _____

Water intake: 🥛🥛🥛🥛🥛🥛🥛🥛🥛🥛

Energy: 🖤🖤🖤🖤🖤

Blood Sugar

		Before	After
Breakfast Time:			
Snack Time:			
Lunch Time:			
Snack Time:			
Dinner Time:			

Vitamins/ Supplements/ Meds:

Sleep (hrs) : _____

Exercise

Notes: _____
_____
_____

Date: _____

Weeks _____

Days _____

Water intake: ⛉ ⛉ ⛉ ⛉ ⛉ ⛉ ⛉

Energy: ♥ ♥ ♥ ♥ ♥

Blood Sugar

		Before	After
Breakfast Time:			
Snack Time:			
Lunch Time:			
Snack Time:			
Dinner Time:			

Vitamins/ Supplements/ Meds:

Sleep (hrs) : _____

Exercise

Notes: _____
_____
_____

Date: _____

Weeks _____
Days _____

Water intake: ⬜⬜⬜⬜⬜⬜⬜

Energy: ♥ ♥ ♥ ♥ ♥

Blood Sugar

		Before	After
Breakfast Time:			
Snack Time:			
Lunch Time:			
Snack Time:			
Dinner Time:			

Vitamins/ Supplements/ Meds:

Sleep (hrs) : _____

Exercise

Notes: _____
_____
_____

Date: _____

Weeks _____
Days _____

Water intake: ⬜⬜⬜⬜⬜⬜⬜

Energy: 💗💗💗💗💗

Blood Sugar

		Before	After
Breakfast Time:			
Snack Time:			
Lunch Time:			
Snack Time:			
Dinner Time:			

Vitamins/ Supplements/ Meds:

Sleep (hrs) : _____

Exercise

Notes: _____

_____

Date: _____

Weeks _____

Days _____

Water intake: 🥛🥛🥛🥛🥛🥛🥛

Energy: 💜💜💜💜💜

Blood Sugar

		Before	After
Breakfast Time:			
Snack Time:			
Lunch Time:			
Snack Time:			
Dinner Time:			

Vitamins/ Supplements/ Meds:

Sleep (hrs) : _____

Exercise

Notes: _____
_____
_____

Date: _____

Weeks _____
Days _____

Water intake: ⎺⎺ ⎺⎺ ⎺⎺ ⎺⎺ ⎺⎺ ⎺⎺ ⎺⎺

Energy: ♥ ♥ ♥ ♥ ♥

		Blood Sugar	
		Before	After
Breakfast Time:			
Snack Time:			
Lunch Time:			
Snack Time:			
Dinner Time:			

Vitamins/ Supplements/ Meds:

Sleep (hrs) : _____

Exercise

Notes: _____
_____
_____

Date: _____

Weeks _____

Days _____

Water intake: ⬜⬜⬜⬜⬜⬜⬜

Energy: 🩶🩶🩶🩶🩶

		Blood Sugar	
		Before	After
Breakfast Time:			
Snack Time:			
Lunch Time:			
Snack Time:			
Dinner Time:			

Vitamins/ Supplements/ Meds:

Sleep (hrs) : _____

Exercise

Notes: _____
_____
_____

Date: _____

Weeks _____

Days _____

Water intake: 🥛🥛🥛🥛🥛🥛🥛

Energy: ♡♡♡♡♡♡

Blood Sugar

		Before	After
Breakfast Time:			
Snack Time:			
Lunch Time:			
Snack Time:			
Dinner Time:			

Vitamins/ Supplements/ Meds:

Sleep (hrs) : _____

Exercise

Notes: _____

Date: _____

Weeks _____
Days _____

Water intake: ⊔ ⊔ ⊔ ⊔ ⊔ ⊔ ⊔ ⊔

Energy: ♥ ♥ ♥ ♥ ♥

Blood Sugar

		Before	After
Breakfast Time:			
Snack Time:			
Lunch Time:			
Snack Time:			
Dinner Time:			

Vitamins/ Supplements/ Meds:

Sleep (hrs) : _____

Exercise

Notes: _____
_____
_____

Date: _____

Weeks _____

Days _____

Water intake: ☐ ☐ ☐ ☐ ☐ ☐ ☐

Energy:

Blood Sugar

		Before	After
Breakfast Time:			
Snack Time:			
Lunch Time:			
Snack Time:			
Dinner Time:			

Vitamins/ Supplements/ Meds:

Sleep (hrs) : _____

Exercise

Notes: _____

Date: _____

Weeks _____

Days _____

Water intake: ⬜⬜⬜⬜⬜⬜⬜

Energy: 🩶🩶🩶🩶🩶🩶🩶

Blood Sugar

		Before	After
Breakfast Time:			
Snack Time:			
Lunch Time:			
Snack Time:			
Dinner Time:			

Vitamins/ Supplements/ Meds:

Sleep (hrs) : _____

Exercise

Notes: _____
_____
_____

Date: _____

Weeks _____

Days _____

Water intake: 🥛 🥛 🥛 🥛 🥛 🥛 🥛 🥛

Energy: ♥ ♥ ♥ ♥ ♥

Blood Sugar

		Before	After
Breakfast Time:			
Snack Time:			
Lunch Time:			
Snack Time:			
Dinner Time:			

Vitamins/ Supplements/ Meds:

Sleep (hrs) : _____

Exercise

Notes:
_____
_____

Date: _____

Weeks _____
Days _____

Water intake: 🥛🥛🥛🥛🥛🥛🥛🥛

Energy: 🩶🩶🩶🩶🩶

		Blood Sugar	
		Before	After
Breakfast Time:			
Snack Time:			
Lunch Time:			
Snack Time:			
Dinner Time:			

Vitamins/ Supplements/ Meds:

Sleep (hrs) : _____

Exercise

Notes: _____
_____

Date: _____

Weeks _____

Days _____

Water intake: 🥛🥛🥛🥛🥛🥛🥛

Energy: ♥ ♥ ♥ ♥ ♥

Blood Sugar

		Before	After
Breakfast Time:			
Snack Time:			
Lunch Time:			
Snack Time:			
Dinner Time:			

Vitamins/ Supplements/ Meds:

Sleep (hrs) : _____

Exercise

Notes: _____

Date: _____

Weeks _____
Days _____

Water intake: 🥛🥛🥛🥛🥛🥛🥛🥛

Energy: 💜💜💜💜💜

Blood Sugar

		Before	After
Breakfast Time:			
Snack Time:			
Lunch Time:			
Snack Time:			
Dinner Time:			

Vitamins/ Supplements/ Meds:

Sleep (hrs) : _____

Exercise

Notes: _____
_____
_____

Date: _____

Weeks _____
Days _____

Water intake: 🥛🥛🥛🥛🥛🥛🥛
Energy: 🖤🖤🖤🖤🖤

Blood Sugar

		Before	After
Breakfast Time:			
Snack Time:			
Lunch Time:			
Snack Time:			
Dinner Time:			

Vitamins/ Supplements/ Meds:

Sleep (hrs) : _____

Exercise

Notes: _____
_____

Date: _____

Weeks _____

Days _____

Water intake: ⌷ ⌷ ⌷ ⌷ ⌷ ⌷ ⌷

Energy: ♥ ♥ ♥ ♥ ♥

Blood Sugar

		Before	After
Breakfast Time:			
Snack Time:			
Lunch Time:			
Snack Time:			
Dinner Time:			

Vitamins/ Supplements/ Meds:

Sleep (hrs) : _____

Exercise

Notes: _____
_____
_____

Date: _____

Weeks _____
Days _____

Water intake: ▯ ▯ ▯ ▯ ▯ ▯ ▯ ▯

Energy: ♥ ♥ ♥ ♥ ♥

Blood Sugar

		Before	After
Breakfast Time:			
Snack Time:			
Lunch Time:			
Snack Time:			
Dinner Time:			

Vitamins/ Supplements/ Meds:

Sleep (hrs) : _____

Exercise

Notes: _____
_____
_____

Date: _____

Weeks _____
Days _____

Water intake:

Energy:

Blood Sugar

		Before	After
Breakfast Time:			
Snack Time:			
Lunch Time:			
Snack Time:			
Dinner Time:			

Vitamins/ Supplements/ Meds:

Sleep (hrs) : _____

Exercise

Notes: _____
_____
_____

Date: _____

Weeks _____
Days _____

Water intake: 🥤🥤🥤🥤🥤🥤🥤

Energy: 💜💜💜💜💜💜

		Blood Sugar	
		Before	After
Breakfast Time:			
Snack Time:			
Lunch Time:			
Snack Time:			
Dinner Time:			

Vitamins/ Supplements/ Meds:

Sleep (hrs) : _____

Exercise

Notes: _____
_____
_____

Date: _____

Weeks _____
Days _____

Water intake: 🥛 🥛 🥛 🥛 🥛 🥛 🥛

Energy: 🖤 🖤 🖤 🖤 🖤

Blood Sugar

		Before	After
Breakfast Time:			
Snack Time:			
Lunch Time:			
Snack Time:			
Dinner Time:			

Vitamins/ Supplements/ Meds:

Sleep (hrs) : _____

Exercise

Notes: _____
_____
_____

Date: _____

Weeks _____
Days _____

Water intake: ⊔ ⊔ ⊔ ⊔ ⊔ ⊔ ⊔

Energy: ♡ ♡ ♡ ♡ ♡

Blood Sugar

		Before	After
Breakfast Time:			
Snack Time:			
Lunch Time:			
Snack Time:			
Dinner Time:			

Vitamins/ Supplements/ Meds:

Sleep (hrs) : _____

Exercise

Notes: _____
_____
_____

Date: _____

Weeks _____
Days _____

Water intake:

Energy:

Blood Sugar

		Before	After
Breakfast Time:			
Snack Time:			
Lunch Time:			
Snack Time:			
Dinner Time:			

Vitamins/ Supplements/ Meds:

Sleep (hrs) : _____

Exercise

Notes: _____

Date: _____

Weeks _____

Days _____

Water intake: ⬜ ⬜ ⬜ ⬜ ⬜ ⬜ ⬜ ⬜

Energy: ♥ ♥ ♥ ♥ ♥

Blood Sugar

		Before	After
Breakfast Time:			
Snack Time:			
Lunch Time:			
Snack Time:			
Dinner Time:			

Vitamins/ Supplements/ Meds:

Sleep (hrs) : _____

Exercise

Notes: _____
_____
_____

Date: _____

Weeks _____
Days _____

Water intake: 🥛🥛🥛🥛🥛🥛🥛🥛

Energy: 💜💜💜💜💜

		Blood Sugar	
		Before	After
Breakfast Time:			
Snack Time:			
Lunch Time:			
Snack Time:			
Dinner Time:			

Vitamins/ Supplements/ Meds:

Sleep (hrs) : _____

Exercise

Notes: _____
_____
_____

Date: _____

Weeks _____

Days _____

Water intake: 🥛 🥛 🥛 🥛 🥛 🥛 🥛

Energy: ♥ ♥ ♥ ♥ ♥

Blood Sugar

		Before	After
Breakfast Time:			
Snack Time:			
Lunch Time:			
Snack Time:			
Dinner Time:			

Vitamins/ Supplements/ Meds:

Sleep (hrs) : _____

Exercise

Notes: _____

Date: _____

Weeks _____
Days _____

Water intake: ⛶ ⛶ ⛶ ⛶ ⛶ ⛶ ⛶

Energy: 🤍 🤍 🤍 🤍 🤍

Blood Sugar

		Before	After
Breakfast Time:			
Snack Time:			
Lunch Time:			
Snack Time:			
Dinner Time:			

Vitamins/ Supplements/ Meds:

Sleep (hrs) : _____

Exercise

Notes: _____
_____
_____

Date: _____

Weeks _____

Days _____

Water intake: ⬚ ⬚ ⬚ ⬚ ⬚ ⬚ ⬚

Energy: ♡ ♡ ♡ ♡ ♡

Blood Sugar

		Before	After
Breakfast Time:			
Snack Time:			
Lunch Time:			
Snack Time:			
Dinner Time:			

Vitamins/ Supplements/ Meds:

Sleep (hrs) : _____

Exercise

Notes:
_____
_____

Date: _____

Weeks _____

Days _____

Water intake: ⬜ ⬜ ⬜ ⬜ ⬜ ⬜ ⬜ ⬜

Energy: 🤍 🤍 🤍 🤍 🤍

Blood Sugar

		Before	After
Breakfast Time:			
Snack Time:			
Lunch Time:			
Snack Time:			
Dinner Time:			

Vitamins/ Supplements/ Meds:

Sleep (hrs) : _____

Exercise

Notes: _____
_____
_____

Date: _____

Weeks _____
Days _____

Water intake: ⊔ ⊔ ⊔ ⊔ ⊔ ⊔ ⊔

Energy: ♥ ♥ ♥ ♥ ♥ ♥

Blood Sugar

		Before	After
Breakfast Time:			
Snack Time:			
Lunch Time:			
Snack Time:			
Dinner Time:			

Vitamins/ Supplements/ Meds:

Sleep (hrs) : _____

Exercise

Notes: _____

_____

Date: _____

Weeks _____
Days _____

Water intake: ⬜ ⬜ ⬜ ⬜ ⬜ ⬜ ⬜

Energy: 🧡 🧡 🧡 🧡 🧡

Blood Sugar

		Before	After
Breakfast Time:			
Snack Time:			
Lunch Time:			
Snack Time:			
Dinner Time:			

Vitamins/ Supplements/ Meds:

Sleep (hrs) : _____

Exercise

Notes:

Date: _____

Weeks _____

Days _____

Water intake: ⬚ ⬚ ⬚ ⬚ ⬚ ⬚ ⬚

Energy: ♡ ♡ ♡ ♡ ♡

Blood Sugar

		Before	After
Breakfast Time:			
Snack Time:			
Lunch Time:			
Snack Time:			
Dinner Time:			

Vitamins/ Supplements/ Meds:

Sleep (hrs) : _____

Exercise

Notes: _____

_____

_____

Date: _____

Weeks _____
Days _____

Water intake: ⬜ ⬜ ⬜ ⬜ ⬜ ⬜ ⬜

Energy: 🤍 🤍 🤍 🤍 🤍

Blood Sugar

		Before	After
Breakfast Time:			
Snack Time:			
Lunch Time:			
Snack Time:			
Dinner Time:			

Vitamins/ Supplements/ Meds:

Sleep (hrs) : _____

Exercise

Notes: _____
_____
_____

Date: _____

Weeks _____
Days _____

Water intake: 🥛🥛🥛🥛🥛🥛🥛🥛

Energy: ♥♥♥♥♥

		Blood Sugar	
		Before	After
Breakfast Time:			
Snack Time:			
Lunch Time:			
Snack Time:			
Dinner Time:			

Vitamins/ Supplements/ Meds:

Sleep (hrs) : _____

Exercise

Notes: _____
_____
_____

Date: _____

Weeks _____

Days _____

Water intake: ⬜ ⬜ ⬜ ⬜ ⬜ ⬜ ⬜ ⬜

Energy: 🩶 🩶 🩶 🩶 🩶 🩶

		Blood Sugar	
		Before	After
Breakfast Time:			
Snack Time:			
Lunch Time:			
Snack Time:			
Dinner Time:			

Vitamins/ Supplements/ Meds:

Sleep (hrs) : _____

Exercise

Notes: _____

_____

_____

Date: _____

Weeks _____
Days _____

Water intake: 🥛🥛🥛🥛🥛🥛🥛

Energy: ♥♥♥♥♥♥

Blood Sugar

		Before	After
Breakfast Time:			
Snack Time:			
Lunch Time:			
Snack Time:			
Dinner Time:			

Vitamins/ Supplements/ Meds:

Sleep (hrs) : _____

Exercise

Notes: _____
_____
_____

Date: _____

Weeks _____
Days _____

Water intake: 🥛🥛🥛🥛🥛🥛🥛🥛

Energy: 💜💜💜💜💜

		Blood Sugar	
		Before	After
Breakfast Time:			
Snack Time:			
Lunch Time:			
Snack Time:			
Dinner Time:			

Vitamins/ Supplements/ Meds:

Sleep (hrs) : _____

Exercise

Notes: _____
_____
_____

Date: _____

Weeks _____
Days _____

Water intake: ⊔ ⊔ ⊔ ⊔ ⊔ ⊔ ⊔

Energy: ♥ ♥ ♥ ♥ ♥

Blood Sugar

		Before	After
Breakfast Time:			
Snack Time:			
Lunch Time:			
Snack Time:			
Dinner Time:			

Vitamins/ Supplements/ Meds:

Sleep (hrs) : _____

Exercise

Notes: _____
_____
_____

Date: _____

Weeks _____
Days _____

Water intake: ⌷ ⌷ ⌷ ⌷ ⌷ ⌷ ⌷

Energy: ♥ ♥ ♥ ♥ ♥

Blood Sugar

		Before	After
Breakfast Time:			
Snack Time:			
Lunch Time:			
Snack Time:			
Dinner Time:			

Vitamins/ Supplements/ Meds:

Sleep (hrs) : _____

Exercise

Notes: _____
_____
_____

Date: _____

Weeks _____

Days _____

Water intake: ⊔ ⊔ ⊔ ⊔ ⊔ ⊔ ⊔

Energy:

Blood Sugar

		Before	After
Breakfast Time:			
Snack Time:			
Lunch Time:			
Snack Time:			
Dinner Time:			

Vitamins/ Supplements/ Meds:

Sleep (hrs) : _____

Exercise

Notes: _____
_____

Date: _____

Weeks _____
Days _____

Water intake: 🥛🥛🥛🥛🥛🥛🥛🥛

Energy: 💜💜💜💜💜

Blood Sugar

		Before	After
Breakfast Time:			
Snack Time:			
Lunch Time:			
Snack Time:			
Dinner Time:			

Vitamins/ Supplements/ Meds:

Sleep (hrs) : _____

Exercise

Notes: _____
_____
_____

Date: _____

Weeks _____

Days _____

Water intake: ⊍ ⊍ ⊍ ⊍ ⊍ ⊍ ⊍

Energy: ♥ ♥ ♥ ♥ ♥

Blood Sugar

		Before	After
Breakfast Time:			
Snack Time:			
Lunch Time:			
Snack Time:			
Dinner Time:			

Vitamins/ Supplements/ Meds:

Sleep (hrs) : _____

Exercise

Notes: _____
_____

Date: _____

Weeks _____
Days _____

Water intake: 🥤🥤🥤🥤🥤🥤🥤

Energy: 🖤🖤🖤🖤🖤

Blood Sugar

		Before	After
Breakfast Time:			
Snack Time:			
Lunch Time:			
Snack Time:			
Dinner Time:			

Vitamins/ Supplements/ Meds:

Sleep (hrs) : _____

Exercise

Notes: _____
_____
_____

Date: _____

Weeks _____

Days _____

Water intake: ▢ ▢ ▢ ▢ ▢ ▢ ▢

Energy: ♥ ♥ ♥ ♥ ♥ ♥

		Blood Sugar	
		Before	After
Breakfast Time:			
Snack Time:			
Lunch Time:			
Snack Time:			
Dinner Time:			

Vitamins/ Supplements/ Meds:

Sleep (hrs) : _____

Exercise

Notes: _____
_____

Date: _____

Weeks _____
Days _____

Water intake: ▯ ▯ ▯ ▯ ▯ ▯ ▯ ▯

Energy: 🤍 🤍 🤍 🤍 🤍

Blood Sugar

		Before	After
Breakfast Time:			
Snack Time:			
Lunch Time:			
Snack Time:			
Dinner Time:			

Vitamins/ Supplements/ Meds:

Sleep (hrs) : _____

Exercise

Notes: _____
_____
_____

Date: _____

Weeks _____

Days _____

Water intake: 🥛🥛🥛🥛🥛🥛🥛

Energy:

Blood Sugar

		Before	After
Breakfast Time:			
Snack Time:			
Lunch Time:			
Snack Time:			
Dinner Time:			

Vitamins/ Supplements/ Meds:

Sleep (hrs) : _____

Exercise

Notes: _____

_____

Date: _____

Weeks _____
Days _____

Water intake: ⬜⬜⬜⬜⬜⬜⬜

Energy: 💔💔💔💔💔

Blood Sugar

		Before	After
Breakfast Time:			
Snack Time:			
Lunch Time:			
Snack Time:			
Dinner Time:			

Vitamins/ Supplements/ Meds:

Sleep (hrs) : _____

Exercise

Notes: _____
_____
_____

Date: _____

Weeks _____

Days _____

Water intake: ☐ ☐ ☐ ☐ ☐ ☐ ☐

Energy: ♡ ♡ ♡ ♡ ♡ ♡

		Blood Sugar	
		Before	After
Breakfast Time:			
Snack Time:			
Lunch Time:			
Snack Time:			
Dinner Time:			

Vitamins/ Supplements/ Meds:

Sleep (hrs) : _____

Exercise

Notes:
_____
_____

Date: _____

Weeks _____
Days _____

Water intake: 🥤🥤🥤🥤🥤🥤🥤🥤

Energy: 🤍🤍🤍🤍🤍

		Blood Sugar	
		Before	After
Breakfast Time:			
Snack Time:			
Lunch Time:			
Snack Time:			
Dinner Time:			

Vitamins/ Supplements/ Meds:

Sleep (hrs) : _____

Exercise

Notes: _____
_____
_____

Date: _____

Weeks _____

Days _____

Water intake: 🥛🥛🥛🥛🥛🥛🥛

Energy:

Blood Sugar

		Before	After
Breakfast Time:			
Snack Time:			
Lunch Time:			
Snack Time:			
Dinner Time:			

Vitamins/ Supplements/ Meds:

Sleep (hrs) : _____

Exercise

Notes: _____

_____

Date: _____

Weeks _____

Days _____

Water intake: ⊔ ⊔ ⊔ ⊔ ⊔ ⊔ ⊔

Energy: ♥ ♥ ♥ ♥ ♥

Blood Sugar

		Before	After
Breakfast Time:			
Snack Time:			
Lunch Time:			
Snack Time:			
Dinner Time:			

Vitamins/ Supplements/ Meds:

Sleep (hrs) : _____

Exercise

Notes: _____
_____
_____

Date: _____

Weeks _____

Days _____

Water intake: ☐ ☐ ☐ ☐ ☐ ☐ ☐

Energy: ♥♥ ♥♥ ♥♥ ♥♥ ♥♥

		Blood Sugar	
		Before	After
Breakfast Time:			
Snack Time:			
Lunch Time:			
Snack Time:			
Dinner Time:			

Vitamins/ Supplements/ Meds:

Sleep (hrs) : _____

Exercise

Notes: _____
_____
_____

Date: _____

Weeks _____

Days _____

Water intake: 🥛🥛🥛🥛🥛🥛🥛

Energy: 🖤 🖤 🖤 🖤 🖤

Blood Sugar

		Before	After
Breakfast Time:			
Snack Time:			
Lunch Time:			
Snack Time:			
Dinner Time:			

Vitamins/ Supplements/ Meds:

Sleep (hrs) : _____

Exercise

Notes: _____

_____

_____

Date: _____

Weeks _____
Days _____

Water intake: ⬜ ⬜ ⬜ ⬜ ⬜ ⬜ ⬜

Energy: 💗 💗 💗 💗 💗

Blood Sugar

		Before	After
Breakfast Time:			
Snack Time:			
Lunch Time:			
Snack Time:			
Dinner Time:			

Vitamins/ Supplements/ Meds:

Sleep (hrs) : _____

Exercise

Notes: _____
_____

Date: _____

Weeks _____
Days _____

Water intake: 🥛🥛🥛🥛🥛🥛🥛

Energy: 💜💜💜💜💜

Blood Sugar

		Before	After
Breakfast Time:			
Snack Time:			
Lunch Time:			
Snack Time:			
Dinner Time:			

Vitamins/ Supplements/ Meds:

Sleep (hrs) : _____

Exercise

Notes: _____
_____
_____

Date: _____

Weeks _____
Days _____

Water intake: ⬚ ⬚ ⬚ ⬚ ⬚ ⬚ ⬚
Energy: ♥ ♥ ♥ ♥ ♥

Blood Sugar

		Before	After
Breakfast Time:			
Snack Time:			
Lunch Time:			
Snack Time:			
Dinner Time:			

Vitamins/ Supplements/ Meds:

Sleep (hrs): _____

Exercise

Notes: _____
_____
_____

Date: _____

Weeks _____
Days _____

Water intake: 🥤🥤🥤🥤🥤🥤🥤

Energy: 💜💜💜💜💜

Blood Sugar

		Before	After
Breakfast Time:			
Snack Time:			
Lunch Time:			
Snack Time:			
Dinner Time:			

Vitamins/ Supplements/ Meds:

Sleep (hrs) : _____

Exercise

Notes: _____
_____
_____

Date: _____

Weeks _____

Water intake: 🥛🥛🥛🥛🥛🥛🥛

Days _____

Energy: ♥♥ ♥♥ ♥♥ ♥♥ ♥♥

		Blood Sugar	
		Before	After
Breakfast Time:			
Snack Time:			
Lunch Time:			
Snack Time:			
Dinner Time:			

Vitamins/ Supplements/ Meds:

Sleep (hrs) : _____

Exercise

Notes:

Date: _____

Weeks _____

Days _____

Water intake: 🥛🥛🥛🥛🥛🥛🥛

Energy: 🩶🩶🩶🩶🩶

Blood Sugar

		Before	After
Breakfast Time:			
Snack Time:			
Lunch Time:			
Snack Time:			
Dinner Time:			

Vitamins/ Supplements/ Meds:

Sleep (hrs) : _____

Exercise

Notes: _____

_____

_____

Date: _____

Weeks _____

Days _____

Water intake: 🥛 🥛 🥛 🥛 🥛 🥛 🥛

Energy: 💜 💜 💜 💜 💜

		Blood Sugar	
		Before	After
Breakfast Time:			
Snack Time:			
Lunch Time:			
Snack Time:			
Dinner Time:			

Vitamins/ Supplements/ Meds:

Sleep (hrs) : _____

Exercise

Notes: _____
_____

Date: _____

Weeks _____
Days _____

Water intake: 🥤🥤🥤🥤🥤🥤🥤

Energy: 🧡🧡🧡🧡🧡

		Blood Sugar	
		Before	After
Breakfast Time:			
Snack Time:			
Lunch Time:			
Snack Time:			
Dinner Time:			

Vitamins/ Supplements/ Meds:

Sleep (hrs) : _____

Exercise

Notes: _____
_____
_____

Date: _____

Weeks _____
Days _____

Water intake: 🥛🥛🥛🥛🥛🥛🥛

Energy: ♥ ♥ ♥ ♥ ♥

Blood Sugar

		Before	After
Breakfast Time:			
Snack Time:			
Lunch Time:			
Snack Time:			
Dinner Time:			

Vitamins/ Supplements/ Meds:

Sleep (hrs) : _____

Exercise

Notes:

Date: _____

Weeks _____

Days _____

Water intake: 🥤🥤🥤🥤🥤🥤🥤

Energy: 💜💜💜💜💜

Blood Sugar

		Before	After
Breakfast Time:			
Snack Time:			
Lunch Time:			
Snack Time:			
Dinner Time:			

Vitamins/ Supplements/ Meds:

Sleep (hrs) : _____

Exercise

Notes: _____
_____
_____

Date: _____

Weeks _____

Days _____

Water intake: ⬠ ⬠ ⬠ ⬠ ⬠ ⬠ ⬠

Energy: ♥ ♥ ♥ ♥ ♥

		Blood Sugar	
		Before	After
Breakfast Time:			
Snack Time:			
Lunch Time:			
Snack Time:			
Dinner Time:			

Vitamins/ Supplements/ Meds:

Sleep (hrs) : _____

Exercise

Notes:

_____

_____

Date: _____

Weeks _____
Days _____

Water intake: 🥛 🥛 🥛 🥛 🥛 🥛

Energy: 💜 💜 💜 💜 💜 💜

Blood Sugar

		Before	After
Breakfast Time:			
Snack Time:			
Lunch Time:			
Snack Time:			
Dinner Time:			

Vitamins/ Supplements/ Meds:

Sleep (hrs) : _____

Exercise

Notes: _____
_____
_____

Date: _____

Weeks _____
Days _____

Water intake: ▯ ▯ ▯ ▯ ▯ ▯ ▯ ▯

Energy: ♥ ♥ ♥ ♥ ♥ ♥

Blood Sugar

		Before	After
Breakfast Time:			
Snack Time:			
Lunch Time:			
Snack Time:			
Dinner Time:			

Vitamins/ Supplements/ Meds:

Sleep (hrs) : _____

Exercise

Notes: _____

Date: _____

Weeks _____
Days _____

Water intake: ⛶ ⛶ ⛶ ⛶ ⛶ ⛶ ⛶

Energy: ♥ ♥ ♥ ♥ ♥

		Blood Sugar	
		Before	After
Breakfast Time:			
Snack Time:			
Lunch Time:			
Snack Time:			
Dinner Time:			

Vitamins/ Supplements/ Meds:

Sleep (hrs) : _____

Exercise

Notes: _____
_____
_____

Date: _____

Weeks _____ **Water intake:** 🥛🥛🥛🥛🥛🥛🥛🥛

Days _____ **Energy:** ♡♡♡♡♡

		Blood Sugar	
		Before	After
Breakfast Time:			
Snack Time:			
Lunch Time:			
Snack Time:			
Dinner Time:			

Vitamins/ Supplements/ Meds:

Sleep (hrs) : _____

Exercise

Notes: _____

Made in United States
Orlando, FL
24 September 2024

51929718R00068